FRACTION MULTIPLICATION AND DIVISION

Math Workbooks Grade 6
Children's Fraction Books

MULTIPLYING FRACTIONS

EXERCISE 1

Directions: Multiply the fractions and write the solution on the space provided.

1) $\dfrac{5}{10} \times \dfrac{1}{2} =$

2) $\dfrac{2}{7} \times \dfrac{9}{10} =$

3) $\dfrac{6}{10} \times \dfrac{1}{2} =$

4) $\dfrac{1}{2} \times \dfrac{2}{4} =$

5) $\dfrac{1}{7} \times \dfrac{1}{2} =$

6) $\dfrac{1}{3} \times \dfrac{4}{5} =$

Directions: Multiply the fractions and write the solution on the space provided.

1) $\dfrac{1}{2} \times \dfrac{3}{6} =$

2) $\dfrac{1}{10} \times \dfrac{3}{5} =$

3) $\dfrac{1}{7} \times \dfrac{4}{6} =$

4) $\dfrac{2}{3} \times \dfrac{1}{2} =$

5) $\dfrac{2}{3} \times \dfrac{4}{9} =$

6) $\dfrac{1}{2} \times \dfrac{2}{4} =$

EXERCISE 3

Directions: Multiply the fractions and write the solution on the space provided.

1) $\dfrac{9}{10} \times \dfrac{2}{4} =$

2) $\dfrac{3}{9} \times \dfrac{1}{5} =$

3) $\dfrac{2}{6} \times \dfrac{1}{3} =$

4) $\dfrac{1}{5} \times \dfrac{2}{8} =$

5) $\dfrac{5}{9} \times \dfrac{3}{5} =$

6) $\dfrac{2}{3} \times \dfrac{7}{10} =$

EXERCISE 4

Directions: Multiply the fractions and write the solution on the space provided.

1) $\dfrac{5}{7} \times \dfrac{7}{8} =$

2) $\dfrac{5}{9} \times \dfrac{1}{4} =$

3) $\dfrac{2}{5} \times \dfrac{8}{9} =$

4) $\dfrac{1}{5} \times \dfrac{2}{10} =$

5) $\dfrac{2}{10} \times \dfrac{2}{6} =$

6) $\dfrac{3}{6} \times \dfrac{1}{2} =$

EXERCISE 5

Directions: Multiply the fractions and write the solution on the space provided.

1) $\dfrac{4}{6} \times \dfrac{2}{10} =$

2) $\dfrac{2}{4} \times \dfrac{2}{6} =$

3) $\dfrac{4}{9} \times \dfrac{6}{7} =$

4) $\dfrac{2}{6} \times \dfrac{2}{3} =$

5) $\dfrac{2}{3} \times \dfrac{4}{5} =$

6) $\dfrac{3}{6} \times \dfrac{1}{3} =$

EXERCISE 6

1) $\dfrac{1}{3} \times \dfrac{3}{4} =$

2) $\dfrac{1}{7} \times \dfrac{1}{3} =$

3) $\dfrac{1}{4} \times \dfrac{5}{7} =$

4) $\dfrac{2}{3} \times \dfrac{2}{4} =$

5) $\dfrac{3}{4} \times \dfrac{1}{8} =$

6) $\dfrac{1}{3} \times \dfrac{1}{4} =$

EXERCISE 7

Directions: Multiply the fractions and write the solution on the space provided.

1) $\dfrac{1}{2} \times \dfrac{2}{6} =$

2) $\dfrac{7}{9} \times \dfrac{2}{3} =$

3) $\dfrac{5}{9} \times \dfrac{1}{2} =$

4) $\dfrac{3}{6} \times \dfrac{1}{7} =$

5) $\dfrac{8}{9} \times \dfrac{3}{5} =$

6) $\dfrac{4}{9} \times \dfrac{2}{7} =$

EXERCISE 8

Directions: Multiply the fractions and write the solution on the space provided.

1) $\dfrac{9}{10} \times \dfrac{3}{6} =$

2) $\dfrac{1}{5} \times \dfrac{6}{10} =$

3) $\dfrac{3}{5} \times \dfrac{3}{8} =$

4) $\dfrac{4}{9} \times \dfrac{2}{5} =$

5) $\dfrac{5}{8} \times \dfrac{1}{2} =$

6) $\dfrac{2}{4} \times \dfrac{6}{9} =$

EXERCISE 9

Directions: Multiply the fractions and write the solution on the space provided.

1) $\dfrac{2}{7} \times \dfrac{1}{2} =$

2) $\dfrac{3}{7} \times \dfrac{1}{5} =$

3) $\dfrac{2}{4} \times \dfrac{3}{6} =$

4) $\dfrac{2}{4} \times \dfrac{2}{3} =$

5) $\dfrac{2}{3} \times \dfrac{1}{10} =$

6) $\dfrac{3}{5} \times \dfrac{5}{6} =$

EXERCISE 10

Directions: Multiply the fractions and write the solution on the space provided.

1) $\dfrac{5}{6} \times \dfrac{6}{8} =$

2) $\dfrac{2}{6} \times \dfrac{1}{3} =$

3) $\dfrac{9}{10} \times \dfrac{5}{9} =$

4) $\dfrac{3}{10} \times \dfrac{2}{4} =$

5) $\dfrac{3}{9} \times \dfrac{1}{3} =$

6) $\dfrac{2}{5} \times \dfrac{1}{2} =$

EXERCISE II

1) $\dfrac{2}{9} \times \dfrac{2}{3} =$

2) $\dfrac{2}{9} \times \dfrac{6}{10} =$

3) $\dfrac{2}{6} \times \dfrac{1}{2} =$

4) $\dfrac{1}{2} \times \dfrac{3}{4} =$

5) $\dfrac{6}{10} \times \dfrac{3}{4} =$

6) $\dfrac{1}{6} \times \dfrac{6}{10} =$

EXERCISE 12

Directions: Multiply the fractions and write the solution on the space provided.

1) $\dfrac{3}{8} \times \dfrac{1}{9} =$

2) $\dfrac{2}{3} \times \dfrac{8}{10} =$

3) $\dfrac{4}{10} \times \dfrac{1}{2} =$

4) $\dfrac{1}{4} \times \dfrac{1}{3} =$

5) $\dfrac{2}{5} \times \dfrac{1}{2} =$

6) $\dfrac{3}{5} \times \dfrac{2}{3} =$

Directions: Multiply the fractions and write the solution on the space provided.

1) $\dfrac{6}{8} \times \dfrac{2}{3} =$

2) $\dfrac{6}{7} \times \dfrac{2}{10} =$

3) $\dfrac{1}{3} \times \dfrac{3}{6} =$

4) $\dfrac{1}{2} \times \dfrac{2}{3} =$

5) $\dfrac{4}{7} \times \dfrac{2}{6} =$

6) $\dfrac{3}{6} \times \dfrac{7}{9} =$

EXERCISE 14

Directions: Multiply the fractions and write the solution on the space provided.

1) $\dfrac{1}{10} \times \dfrac{1}{3} =$

2) $\dfrac{3}{7} \times \dfrac{1}{2} =$

3) $\dfrac{2}{4} \times \dfrac{3}{7} =$

4) $\dfrac{7}{8} \times \dfrac{4}{7} =$

5) $\dfrac{5}{7} \times \dfrac{1}{3} =$

6) $\dfrac{3}{6} \times \dfrac{6}{9} =$

EXERCISE 15

Directions: Multiply the fractions and write the solution on the space provided.

1) $\dfrac{4}{5} \times \dfrac{4}{8} =$

2) $\dfrac{2}{10} \times \dfrac{2}{6} =$

3) $\dfrac{1}{4} \times \dfrac{8}{10} =$

4) $\dfrac{6}{8} \times \dfrac{5}{6} =$

5) $\dfrac{9}{10} \times \dfrac{1}{2} =$

6) $\dfrac{1}{8} \times \dfrac{1}{6} =$

EXERCISE 16

Directions: Multiply the fractions and write the solution on the space provided.

1) $\dfrac{1}{3} \times \dfrac{2}{7} =$

2) $\dfrac{9}{10} \times \dfrac{4}{7} =$

3) $\dfrac{1}{8} \times \dfrac{1}{2} =$

4) $\dfrac{5}{6} \times \dfrac{2}{10} =$

5) $\dfrac{4}{6} \times \dfrac{2}{7} =$

6) $\dfrac{5}{6} \times \dfrac{1}{3} =$

Directions: Multiply the fractions and write the solution on the space provided.

1) $\dfrac{3}{10} \times \dfrac{1}{9} =$

2) $\dfrac{4}{6} \times \dfrac{5}{9} =$

3) $\dfrac{5}{9} \times \dfrac{1}{2} =$

4) $\dfrac{3}{5} \times \dfrac{1}{4} =$

5) $\dfrac{6}{7} \times \dfrac{2}{10} =$

6) $\dfrac{6}{7} \times \dfrac{4}{5} =$

EXERCISE 18

Directions: Multiply the fractions and write the solution on the space provided.

1) $\dfrac{1}{3} \times \dfrac{1}{2} =$

2) $\dfrac{7}{10} \times \dfrac{2}{7} =$

3) $\dfrac{1}{2} \times \dfrac{4}{7} =$

4) $\dfrac{5}{8} \times \dfrac{4}{9} =$

5) $\dfrac{7}{10} \times \dfrac{4}{7} =$

6) $\dfrac{4}{6} \times \dfrac{2}{4} =$

EXERCISE 19

 Multiply the fractions and write the solution on the space provided.

1) $\dfrac{9}{10} \times \dfrac{2}{3} =$

2) $\dfrac{5}{10} \times \dfrac{3}{7} =$

3) $\dfrac{2}{4} \times \dfrac{1}{2} =$

4) $\dfrac{1}{8} \times \dfrac{5}{10} =$

5) $\dfrac{8}{9} \times \dfrac{1}{2} =$

6) $\dfrac{3}{8} \times \dfrac{4}{9} =$

EXERCISE 20

Directions: Multiply the fractions and write the solution on the space provided.

1) $\dfrac{3}{4} \times \dfrac{5}{7} =$

2) $\dfrac{3}{6} \times \dfrac{2}{8} =$

3) $\dfrac{1}{3} \times \dfrac{4}{8} =$

4) $\dfrac{2}{3} \times \dfrac{1}{7} =$

5) $\dfrac{3}{4} \times \dfrac{2}{3} =$

6) $\dfrac{2}{4} \times \dfrac{2}{8} =$

Directions: Multiply the fractions and write the solution on the space provided.

1) $\dfrac{8}{9} \times \dfrac{16}{20} =$

2) $\dfrac{11}{18} \times \dfrac{1}{7} =$

3) $\dfrac{3}{4} \times \dfrac{17}{18} =$

4) $\dfrac{5}{6} \times \dfrac{5}{8} =$

5) $\dfrac{11}{12} \times \dfrac{13}{14} =$

6) $\dfrac{1}{8} \times \dfrac{3}{5} =$

EXERCISE 22

Directions: Multiply the fractions and write the solution on the space provided.

1) $\dfrac{7}{12} \times \dfrac{1}{2} =$

2) $\dfrac{1}{7} \times \dfrac{2}{15} =$

3) $\dfrac{7}{18} \times \dfrac{1}{5} =$

4) $\dfrac{8}{18} \times \dfrac{4}{9} =$

5) $\dfrac{5}{8} \times \dfrac{2}{4} =$

6) $\dfrac{1}{2} \times \dfrac{3}{5} =$

EXERCISE 23

Directions: Multiply the fractions and write the solution on the space provided.

1) $\dfrac{7}{14} \times \dfrac{1}{2} =$

2) $\dfrac{1}{3} \times \dfrac{13}{16} =$

3) $\dfrac{4}{8} \times \dfrac{5}{14} =$

4) $\dfrac{1}{2} \times \dfrac{9}{14} =$

5) $\dfrac{1}{2} \times \dfrac{6}{7} =$

6) $\dfrac{3}{18} \times \dfrac{11}{20} =$

EXERCISE 24

Directions: Multiply the fractions and write the solution on the space provided.

1) $\dfrac{2}{4} \times \dfrac{4}{8} =$

2) $\dfrac{4}{5} \times \dfrac{5}{6} =$

3) $\dfrac{1}{2} \times \dfrac{2}{3} =$

4) $\dfrac{14}{20} \times \dfrac{10}{16} =$

5) $\dfrac{1}{4} \times \dfrac{1}{5} =$

6) $\dfrac{14}{16} \times \dfrac{10}{12} =$

EXERCISE 25

Directions: Multiply the fractions and write the solution on the space provided.

1) $\dfrac{19}{20} \times \dfrac{6}{7} =$

2) $\dfrac{1}{3} \times \dfrac{1}{5} =$

3) $\dfrac{9}{10} \times \dfrac{1}{2} =$

4) $\dfrac{5}{9} \times \dfrac{5}{14} =$

5) $\dfrac{6}{14} \times \dfrac{6}{9} =$

6) $\dfrac{6}{9} \times \dfrac{1}{2} =$

EXERCISE 26

Directions: Multiply the fractions and write the solution on the space provided.

1) $\dfrac{3}{10} \times \dfrac{2}{7} =$

2) $\dfrac{2}{5} \times \dfrac{2}{6} =$

3) $\dfrac{2}{5} \times \dfrac{1}{2} =$

4) $\dfrac{1}{2} \times \dfrac{2}{5} =$

5) $\dfrac{1}{2} \times \dfrac{6}{15} =$

6) $\dfrac{1}{2} \times \dfrac{2}{4} =$

EXERCISE 27

Directions: Multiply the fractions and write the solution on the space provided.

1) $\dfrac{2}{3} \times \dfrac{5}{6} =$

2) $\dfrac{11}{14} \times \dfrac{4}{15} =$

3) $\dfrac{3}{14} \times \dfrac{6}{7} =$

4) $\dfrac{1}{10} \times \dfrac{9}{20} =$

5) $\dfrac{8}{16} \times \dfrac{1}{4} =$

6) $\dfrac{13}{18} \times \dfrac{7}{10} =$

EXERCISE 28

Directions: Multiply the fractions and write the solution on the space provided.

1) $\dfrac{6}{12} \times \dfrac{4}{6} =$

2) $\dfrac{6}{7} \times \dfrac{1}{14} =$

3) $\dfrac{2}{4} \times \dfrac{1}{3} =$

4) $\dfrac{3}{10} \times \dfrac{4}{8} =$

5) $\dfrac{13}{15} \times \dfrac{3}{6} =$

6) $\dfrac{1}{3} \times \dfrac{17}{20} =$

EXERCISE 29

Directions: Multiply the fractions and write the solution on the space provided.

1) $\dfrac{7}{8} \times \dfrac{1}{2} =$

2) $\dfrac{4}{18} \times \dfrac{10}{15} =$

3) $\dfrac{6}{7} \times \dfrac{1}{2} =$

4) $\dfrac{3}{6} \times \dfrac{5}{10} =$

5) $\dfrac{3}{4} \times \dfrac{7}{18} =$

6) $\dfrac{4}{6} \times \dfrac{11}{20} =$

EXERCISE 30

Directions: Multiply the fractions and write the solution on the space provided.

1) $\dfrac{1}{2} \times \dfrac{8}{9} =$

2) $\dfrac{1}{7} \times \dfrac{2}{8} =$

3) $\dfrac{12}{14} \times \dfrac{2}{3} =$

4) $\dfrac{1}{2} \times \dfrac{1}{14} =$

5) $\dfrac{7}{20} \times \dfrac{3}{8} =$

6) $\dfrac{2}{3} \times \dfrac{5}{8} =$

DIVIDING FRACTIONS

Directions: Divide the fractions and write the solution on the space provided.

1) $\dfrac{9}{14} \div \dfrac{5}{7} =$

2) $\dfrac{1}{2} \div \dfrac{1}{3} =$

3) $\dfrac{6}{16} \div \dfrac{4}{10} =$

4) $\dfrac{7}{15} \div \dfrac{3}{6} =$

5) $\dfrac{8}{14} \div \dfrac{2}{3} =$

6) $\dfrac{3}{4} \div \dfrac{1}{3} =$

EXERCISE 2

Directions: Divide the fractions and write the solution on the space provided.

1) $\dfrac{7}{10} \div \dfrac{13}{14} =$

2) $\dfrac{2}{7} \div \dfrac{6}{9} =$

3) $\dfrac{1}{9} \div \dfrac{5}{8} =$

4) $\dfrac{2}{4} \div \dfrac{1}{7} =$

5) $\dfrac{1}{6} \div \dfrac{1}{3} =$

6) $\dfrac{5}{7} \div \dfrac{19}{20} =$

EXERCISE 3

Directions: Divide the fractions and write the solution on the space provided.

1) $\dfrac{1}{6} \div \dfrac{1}{9} =$

2) $\dfrac{1}{5} \div \dfrac{6}{15} =$

3) $\dfrac{2}{3} \div \dfrac{1}{2} =$

4) $\dfrac{1}{2} \div \dfrac{1}{9} =$

5) $\dfrac{3}{18} \div \dfrac{1}{2} =$

6) $\dfrac{2}{3} \div \dfrac{11}{16} =$

EXERCISE 4

Directions: Divide the fractions and write the solution on the space provided.

1) $\dfrac{4}{8} \div \dfrac{7}{10} =$

2) $\dfrac{8}{10} \div \dfrac{6}{12} =$

3) $\dfrac{1}{4} \div \dfrac{6}{7} =$

4) $\dfrac{16}{20} \div \dfrac{1}{8} =$

5) $\dfrac{7}{9} \div \dfrac{17}{20} =$

6) $\dfrac{14}{15} \div \dfrac{4}{10} =$

EXERCISE 5

Directions: Divide the fractions and write the solution on the space provided.

1) $\dfrac{3}{5} \div \dfrac{1}{4} =$

2) $\dfrac{2}{9} \div \dfrac{2}{5} =$

3) $\dfrac{6}{15} \div \dfrac{1}{2} =$

4) $\dfrac{9}{12} \div \dfrac{3}{6} =$

5) $\dfrac{10}{12} \div \dfrac{1}{2} =$

6) $\dfrac{1}{2} \div \dfrac{1}{20} =$

EXERCISE 6

Directions: Divide the fractions and write the solution on the space provided.

1) $\dfrac{7}{9} \div \dfrac{1}{3} =$

2) $\dfrac{2}{7} \div \dfrac{2}{4} =$

3) $\dfrac{8}{16} \div \dfrac{16}{18} =$

4) $\dfrac{2}{10} \div \dfrac{1}{14} =$

5) $\dfrac{7}{12} \div \dfrac{8}{16} =$

6) $\dfrac{2}{3} \div \dfrac{1}{4} =$

EXERCISE 7

Directions: Divide the fractions and write the solution on the space provided.

1) $\dfrac{1}{16} \div \dfrac{3}{8} =$

2) $\dfrac{1}{8} \div \dfrac{5}{14} =$

3) $\dfrac{5}{6} \div \dfrac{3}{5} =$

4) $\dfrac{2}{6} \div \dfrac{1}{2} =$

5) $\dfrac{6}{12} \div \dfrac{3}{7} =$

6) $\dfrac{1}{3} \div \dfrac{4}{8} =$

EXERCISE 8

Directions: Divide the fractions and write the solution on the space provided.

1) $\dfrac{7}{8} \div \dfrac{6}{9} =$

2) $\dfrac{7}{14} \div \dfrac{3}{8} =$

3) $\dfrac{2}{14} \div \dfrac{4}{8} =$

4) $\dfrac{10}{18} \div \dfrac{5}{12} =$

5) $\dfrac{9}{10} \div \dfrac{6}{12} =$

6) $\dfrac{7}{16} \div \dfrac{3}{4} =$

EXERCISE 9

Directions: Divide the fractions and write the solution on the space provided.

1) $\dfrac{2}{4} \div \dfrac{3}{14} =$

2) $\dfrac{1}{6} \div \dfrac{17}{18} =$

3) $\dfrac{5}{8} \div \dfrac{2}{14} =$

4) $\dfrac{1}{5} \div \dfrac{1}{7} =$

5) $\dfrac{2}{3} \div \dfrac{3}{16} =$

6) $\dfrac{15}{16} \div \dfrac{3}{5} =$

EXERCISE 10

Directions: Divide the fractions and write the solution on the space provided.

1) $\dfrac{13}{14} \div \dfrac{1}{2} =$

2) $\dfrac{12}{14} \div \dfrac{1}{2} =$

3) $\dfrac{1}{2} \div \dfrac{13}{15} =$

4) $\dfrac{1}{16} \div \dfrac{4}{10} =$

5) $\dfrac{1}{4} \div \dfrac{5}{12} =$

6) $\dfrac{7}{20} \div \dfrac{1}{2} =$

EXERCISE II

Directions: Divide the fractions and write the solution on the space provided.

1) $\dfrac{9}{15} \div \dfrac{6}{7} =$

2) $\dfrac{8}{9} \div \dfrac{1}{3} =$

3) $\dfrac{2}{7} \div \dfrac{2}{8} =$

4) $\dfrac{2}{12} \div \dfrac{4}{6} =$

5) $\dfrac{5}{12} \div \dfrac{4}{8} =$

6) $\dfrac{7}{8} \div \dfrac{2}{3} =$

# EXERCISE 12

Directions: Divide the fractions and write the solution on the space provided.

1) $\dfrac{5}{10} \div \dfrac{4}{7} =$

2) $\dfrac{1}{2} \div \dfrac{12}{16} =$

3) $\dfrac{3}{9} \div \dfrac{4}{10} =$

4) $\dfrac{2}{15} \div \dfrac{1}{5} =$

5) $\dfrac{6}{9} \div \dfrac{2}{4} =$

6) $\dfrac{1}{3} \div \dfrac{6}{8} =$

EXERCISE 13

Directions: Divide the fractions and write the solution on the space provided.

1) $\dfrac{17}{20} \div \dfrac{1}{3} =$

2) $\dfrac{1}{2} \div \dfrac{5}{6} =$

3) $\dfrac{1}{8} \div \dfrac{6}{12} =$

4) $\dfrac{14}{16} \div \dfrac{2}{5} =$

5) $\dfrac{12}{15} \div \dfrac{3}{14} =$

6) $\dfrac{5}{16} \div \dfrac{1}{4} =$

EXERCISE 14

Directions: Divide the fractions and write the solution on the space provided.

1) $\dfrac{4}{6} \div \dfrac{13}{16} =$

2) $\dfrac{3}{6} \div \dfrac{4}{9} =$

3) $\dfrac{7}{15} \div \dfrac{9}{10} =$

4) $\dfrac{14}{18} \div \dfrac{1}{12} =$

5) $\dfrac{9}{14} \div \dfrac{1}{12} =$

6) $\dfrac{11}{16} \div \dfrac{8}{10} =$

EXERCISE 15

Directions: Divide the fractions and write the solution on the space provided.

1) $\dfrac{18}{20} \div \dfrac{8}{15} =$

2) $\dfrac{6}{20} \div \dfrac{3}{4} =$

3) $\dfrac{4}{9} \div \dfrac{1}{14} =$

4) $\dfrac{1}{6} \div \dfrac{6}{8} =$

5) $\dfrac{12}{20} \div \dfrac{1}{16} =$

6) $\dfrac{1}{6} \div \dfrac{7}{9} =$

EXERCISE 16

Directions: Divide the fractions and write the solution on the space provided.

1) $\dfrac{1}{6} \div \dfrac{18}{20} =$

2) $\dfrac{7}{14} \div \dfrac{12}{15} =$

3) $\dfrac{1}{6} \div \dfrac{4}{12} =$

4) $\dfrac{2}{8} \div \dfrac{2}{9} =$

5) $\dfrac{5}{6} \div \dfrac{8}{9} =$

6) $\dfrac{8}{15} \div \dfrac{1}{2} =$

EXERCISE 17

Directions: Divide the fractions and write the solution on the space provided.

1) $\dfrac{5}{12} \div \dfrac{1}{6} =$

2) $\dfrac{3}{16} \div \dfrac{5}{10} =$

3) $\dfrac{6}{10} \div \dfrac{2}{6} =$

4) $\dfrac{1}{10} \div \dfrac{2}{7} =$

5) $\dfrac{3}{5} \div \dfrac{4}{6} =$

6) $\dfrac{7}{9} \div \dfrac{17}{20} =$

ANSWERS

MULTIPLYING FRACTIONS

EXERCISE 1

1) $\dfrac{5}{10} \times \dfrac{1}{2} = \dfrac{5 \times 1}{10 \times 2} = \dfrac{5}{20} = \dfrac{1}{4}$

2) $\dfrac{2}{7} \times \dfrac{9}{10} = \dfrac{2 \times 9}{7 \times 10} = \dfrac{18}{70} = \dfrac{9}{35}$

3) $\dfrac{6}{10} \times \dfrac{1}{2} = \dfrac{6 \times 1}{10 \times 2} = \dfrac{6}{20} = \dfrac{3}{10}$

4) $\dfrac{1}{2} \times \dfrac{2}{4} = \dfrac{1 \times 2}{2 \times 4} = \dfrac{2}{8} = \dfrac{1}{4}$

5) $\dfrac{1}{7} \times \dfrac{1}{2} = \dfrac{1 \times 1}{7 \times 2} = \dfrac{1}{14}$

6) $\dfrac{1}{3} \times \dfrac{4}{5} = \dfrac{1 \times 4}{3 \times 5} = \dfrac{4}{15}$

EXERCISE 2

1) $\dfrac{1}{2} \times \dfrac{3}{6} = \dfrac{1 \times 3}{2 \times 6} = \dfrac{3}{12} = \dfrac{1}{4}$

2) $\dfrac{1}{10} \times \dfrac{3}{5} = \dfrac{1 \times 3}{10 \times 5} = \dfrac{3}{50}$

3) $\dfrac{1}{7} \times \dfrac{4}{6} = \dfrac{1 \times 4}{7 \times 6} = \dfrac{4}{42} = \dfrac{2}{21}$

4) $\dfrac{2}{3} \times \dfrac{1}{2} = \dfrac{2 \times 1}{3 \times 2} = \dfrac{2}{6} = \dfrac{1}{3}$

5) $\dfrac{2}{3} \times \dfrac{4}{9} = \dfrac{2 \times 4}{3 \times 9} = \dfrac{8}{27}$

6) $\dfrac{1}{2} \times \dfrac{2}{4} = \dfrac{1 \times 2}{2 \times 4} = \dfrac{2}{8} = \dfrac{1}{4}$

EXERCISE 3

1) $\dfrac{9}{10} \times \dfrac{2}{4} = \dfrac{9 \times 2}{10 \times 4} = \dfrac{18}{40} = \dfrac{9}{20}$

2) $\dfrac{3}{9} \times \dfrac{1}{5} = \dfrac{3 \times 1}{9 \times 5} = \dfrac{3}{45} = \dfrac{1}{15}$

3) $\dfrac{2}{6} \times \dfrac{1}{3} = \dfrac{2 \times 1}{6 \times 3} = \dfrac{2}{18} = \dfrac{1}{9}$

4) $\dfrac{1}{5} \times \dfrac{2}{8} = \dfrac{1 \times 2}{5 \times 8} = \dfrac{2}{40} = \dfrac{1}{20}$

5) $\dfrac{5}{9} \times \dfrac{3}{5} = \dfrac{5 \times 3}{9 \times 5} = \dfrac{15}{45} = \dfrac{1}{3}$

6) $\dfrac{2}{3} \times \dfrac{7}{10} = \dfrac{2 \times 7}{3 \times 10} = \dfrac{14}{30} = \dfrac{7}{15}$

EXERCISE 4

1) $\dfrac{5}{7} \times \dfrac{7}{8} = \dfrac{5 \times 7}{7 \times 8} = \dfrac{35}{56} = \dfrac{5}{8}$

2) $\dfrac{5}{9} \times \dfrac{1}{4} = \dfrac{5 \times 1}{9 \times 4} = \dfrac{5}{36}$

3) $\dfrac{2}{5} \times \dfrac{8}{9} = \dfrac{2 \times 8}{5 \times 9} = \dfrac{16}{45}$

4) $\dfrac{1}{5} \times \dfrac{2}{10} = \dfrac{1 \times 2}{5 \times 10} = \dfrac{2}{50} = \dfrac{1}{25}$

5) $\dfrac{2}{10} \times \dfrac{2}{6} = \dfrac{2 \times 2}{10 \times 6} = \dfrac{4}{60} = \dfrac{1}{15}$

6) $\dfrac{3}{6} \times \dfrac{1}{2} = \dfrac{3 \times 1}{6 \times 2} = \dfrac{3}{12} = \dfrac{1}{4}$

EXERCISE 5

1) $\dfrac{4}{6} \times \dfrac{2}{10} = \dfrac{4 \times 2}{6 \times 10} = \dfrac{8}{60} = \dfrac{2}{15}$

2) $\dfrac{2}{4} \times \dfrac{2}{6} = \dfrac{2 \times 2}{4 \times 6} = \dfrac{4}{24} = \dfrac{1}{6}$

3) $\dfrac{4}{9} \times \dfrac{6}{7} = \dfrac{4 \times 6}{9 \times 7} = \dfrac{24}{63} = \dfrac{8}{21}$

4) $\dfrac{2}{6} \times \dfrac{2}{3} = \dfrac{2 \times 2}{6 \times 3} = \dfrac{4}{18} = \dfrac{2}{9}$

5) $\dfrac{2}{3} \times \dfrac{4}{5} = \dfrac{2 \times 4}{3 \times 5} = \dfrac{8}{15}$

6) $\dfrac{3}{6} \times \dfrac{1}{3} = \dfrac{3 \times 1}{6 \times 3} = \dfrac{3}{18} = \dfrac{1}{6}$

EXERCISE 6

1) $\dfrac{1}{3} \times \dfrac{3}{4} = \dfrac{1 \times 3}{3 \times 4} = \dfrac{3}{12} = \dfrac{1}{4}$

2) $\dfrac{1}{7} \times \dfrac{1}{3} = \dfrac{1 \times 1}{7 \times 3} = \dfrac{1}{21}$

3) $\dfrac{1}{4} \times \dfrac{5}{7} = \dfrac{1 \times 5}{4 \times 7} = \dfrac{5}{28}$

4) $\dfrac{2}{3} \times \dfrac{2}{4} = \dfrac{2 \times 2}{3 \times 4} = \dfrac{4}{12} = \dfrac{1}{3}$

5) $\dfrac{3}{4} \times \dfrac{1}{8} = \dfrac{3 \times 1}{4 \times 8} = \dfrac{3}{32}$

6) $\dfrac{1}{3} \times \dfrac{1}{4} = \dfrac{1 \times 1}{3 \times 4} = \dfrac{1}{12}$

EXERCISE 7

1) $\dfrac{1}{2} \times \dfrac{2}{6} = \dfrac{1 \times 2}{2 \times 6} = \dfrac{2}{12} = \dfrac{1}{6}$

2) $\dfrac{7}{9} \times \dfrac{2}{3} = \dfrac{7 \times 2}{9 \times 3} = \dfrac{14}{27}$

3) $\dfrac{5}{9} \times \dfrac{1}{2} = \dfrac{5 \times 1}{9 \times 2} = \dfrac{5}{18}$

4) $\dfrac{3}{6} \times \dfrac{1}{7} = \dfrac{3 \times 1}{6 \times 7} = \dfrac{3}{42} = \dfrac{1}{14}$

5) $\dfrac{8}{9} \times \dfrac{3}{5} = \dfrac{8 \times 3}{9 \times 5} = \dfrac{24}{45} = \dfrac{8}{15}$

6) $\dfrac{4}{9} \times \dfrac{2}{7} = \dfrac{4 \times 2}{9 \times 7} = \dfrac{8}{63}$

EXERCISE 8

1) $\dfrac{9}{10} \times \dfrac{3}{6} = \dfrac{9 \times 3}{10 \times 6} = \dfrac{27}{60} = \dfrac{9}{20}$

2) $\dfrac{1}{5} \times \dfrac{6}{10} = \dfrac{1 \times 6}{5 \times 10} = \dfrac{6}{50} = \dfrac{3}{25}$

3) $\dfrac{3}{5} \times \dfrac{3}{8} = \dfrac{3 \times 3}{5 \times 8} = \dfrac{9}{40}$

4) $\dfrac{4}{9} \times \dfrac{2}{5} = \dfrac{4 \times 2}{9 \times 5} = \dfrac{8}{45}$

5) $\dfrac{5}{8} \times \dfrac{1}{2} = \dfrac{5 \times 1}{8 \times 2} = \dfrac{5}{16}$

6) $\dfrac{2}{4} \times \dfrac{6}{9} = \dfrac{2 \times 6}{4 \times 9} = \dfrac{12}{36} = \dfrac{1}{3}$

EXERCISE 9

1) $\dfrac{2}{7} \times \dfrac{1}{2} = \dfrac{2 \times 1}{7 \times 2} = \dfrac{2}{14} = \dfrac{1}{7}$

2) $\dfrac{3}{7} \times \dfrac{1}{5} = \dfrac{3 \times 1}{7 \times 5} = \dfrac{3}{35}$

3) $\dfrac{2}{4} \times \dfrac{3}{6} = \dfrac{2 \times 3}{4 \times 6} = \dfrac{6}{24} = \dfrac{1}{4}$

4) $\dfrac{2}{4} \times \dfrac{2}{3} = \dfrac{2 \times 2}{4 \times 3} = \dfrac{4}{12} = \dfrac{1}{3}$

5) $\dfrac{2}{3} \times \dfrac{1}{10} = \dfrac{2 \times 1}{3 \times 10} = \dfrac{2}{30} = \dfrac{1}{15}$

6) $\dfrac{3}{5} \times \dfrac{5}{6} = \dfrac{3 \times 5}{5 \times 6} = \dfrac{15}{30} = \dfrac{1}{2}$

EXERCISE 10

1) $\dfrac{5}{6} \times \dfrac{6}{8} = \dfrac{5 \times 6}{6 \times 8} = \dfrac{30}{48} = \dfrac{5}{8}$

2) $\dfrac{2}{6} \times \dfrac{1}{3} = \dfrac{2 \times 1}{6 \times 3} = \dfrac{2}{18} = \dfrac{1}{9}$

3) $\dfrac{9}{10} \times \dfrac{5}{9} = \dfrac{9 \times 5}{10 \times 9} = \dfrac{45}{90} = \dfrac{1}{2}$

4) $\dfrac{3}{10} \times \dfrac{2}{4} = \dfrac{3 \times 2}{10 \times 4} = \dfrac{6}{40} = \dfrac{3}{20}$

5) $\dfrac{3}{9} \times \dfrac{1}{3} = \dfrac{3 \times 1}{9 \times 3} = \dfrac{3}{27} = \dfrac{1}{9}$

6) $\dfrac{2}{5} \times \dfrac{1}{2} = \dfrac{2 \times 1}{5 \times 2} = \dfrac{2}{10} = \dfrac{1}{5}$

EXERCISE 11

1) $\dfrac{2}{9} \times \dfrac{2}{3} = \dfrac{2 \times 2}{9 \times 3} = \dfrac{4}{27}$

2) $\dfrac{2}{9} \times \dfrac{6}{10} = \dfrac{2 \times 6}{9 \times 10} = \dfrac{12}{90} = \dfrac{2}{15}$

3) $\dfrac{2}{6} \times \dfrac{1}{2} = \dfrac{2 \times 1}{6 \times 2} = \dfrac{2}{12} = \dfrac{1}{6}$

4) $\dfrac{1}{2} \times \dfrac{3}{4} = \dfrac{1 \times 3}{2 \times 4} = \dfrac{3}{8}$

5) $\dfrac{6}{10} \times \dfrac{3}{4} = \dfrac{6 \times 3}{10 \times 4} = \dfrac{18}{40} = \dfrac{9}{20}$

6) $\dfrac{1}{6} \times \dfrac{6}{10} = \dfrac{1 \times 6}{6 \times 10} = \dfrac{6}{60} = \dfrac{1}{10}$

EXERCISE 12

1) $\dfrac{3}{8} \times \dfrac{1}{9} = \dfrac{3 \times 1}{8 \times 9} = \dfrac{3}{72} = \dfrac{1}{24}$

2) $\dfrac{2}{3} \times \dfrac{8}{10} = \dfrac{2 \times 8}{3 \times 10} = \dfrac{16}{30} = \dfrac{8}{15}$

3) $\dfrac{4}{10} \times \dfrac{1}{2} = \dfrac{4 \times 1}{10 \times 2} = \dfrac{4}{20} = \dfrac{1}{5}$

4) $\dfrac{1}{4} \times \dfrac{1}{3} = \dfrac{1 \times 1}{4 \times 3} = \dfrac{1}{12}$

5) $\dfrac{2}{5} \times \dfrac{1}{2} = \dfrac{2 \times 1}{5 \times 2} = \dfrac{2}{10} = \dfrac{1}{5}$

6) $\dfrac{3}{5} \times \dfrac{2}{3} = \dfrac{3 \times 2}{5 \times 3} = \dfrac{6}{15} = \dfrac{2}{5}$

EXERCISE 13

1) $\dfrac{6}{8} \times \dfrac{2}{3} = \dfrac{6 \times 2}{8 \times 3} = \dfrac{12}{24} = \dfrac{1}{2}$

2) $\dfrac{6}{7} \times \dfrac{2}{10} = \dfrac{6 \times 2}{7 \times 10} = \dfrac{12}{70} = \dfrac{6}{35}$

3) $\dfrac{1}{3} \times \dfrac{3}{6} = \dfrac{1 \times 3}{3 \times 6} = \dfrac{3}{18} = \dfrac{1}{6}$

4) $\dfrac{1}{2} \times \dfrac{2}{3} = \dfrac{1 \times 2}{2 \times 3} = \dfrac{2}{6} = \dfrac{1}{3}$

5) $\dfrac{4}{7} \times \dfrac{2}{6} = \dfrac{4 \times 2}{7 \times 6} = \dfrac{8}{42} = \dfrac{4}{21}$

6) $\dfrac{3}{6} \times \dfrac{7}{9} = \dfrac{3 \times 7}{6 \times 9} = \dfrac{21}{54} = \dfrac{7}{18}$

EXERCISE 14

1) $\dfrac{1}{10} \times \dfrac{1}{3} = \dfrac{1 \times 1}{10 \times 3} = \dfrac{1}{30}$

2) $\dfrac{3}{7} \times \dfrac{1}{2} = \dfrac{3 \times 1}{7 \times 2} = \dfrac{3}{14}$

3) $\dfrac{2}{4} \times \dfrac{3}{7} = \dfrac{2 \times 3}{4 \times 7} = \dfrac{6}{28} = \dfrac{3}{14}$

4) $\dfrac{7}{8} \times \dfrac{4}{7} = \dfrac{7 \times 4}{8 \times 7} = \dfrac{28}{56} = \dfrac{1}{2}$

5) $\dfrac{5}{7} \times \dfrac{1}{3} = \dfrac{5 \times 1}{7 \times 3} = \dfrac{5}{21}$

6) $\dfrac{3}{6} \times \dfrac{6}{9} = \dfrac{3 \times 6}{6 \times 9} = \dfrac{18}{54} = \dfrac{1}{3}$

EXERCISE 15

1) $\dfrac{4}{5} \times \dfrac{4}{8} = \dfrac{4 \times 4}{5 \times 8} = \dfrac{16}{40} = \dfrac{2}{5}$

2) $\dfrac{2}{10} \times \dfrac{2}{6} = \dfrac{2 \times 2}{10 \times 6} = \dfrac{4}{60} = \dfrac{1}{15}$

3) $\dfrac{1}{4} \times \dfrac{8}{10} = \dfrac{1 \times 8}{4 \times 10} = \dfrac{8}{40} = \dfrac{1}{5}$

4) $\dfrac{6}{8} \times \dfrac{5}{6} = \dfrac{6 \times 5}{8 \times 6} = \dfrac{30}{48} = \dfrac{5}{8}$

5) $\dfrac{9}{10} \times \dfrac{1}{2} = \dfrac{9 \times 1}{10 \times 2} = \dfrac{9}{20}$

6) $\dfrac{1}{8} \times \dfrac{1}{6} = \dfrac{1 \times 1}{8 \times 6} = \dfrac{1}{48}$

<h2 style="text-align:center">EXERCISE 16</h2>

1) $\dfrac{1}{3} \times \dfrac{2}{7} = \dfrac{1 \times 2}{3 \times 7} = \dfrac{2}{21}$

2) $\dfrac{9}{10} \times \dfrac{4}{7} = \dfrac{9 \times 4}{10 \times 7} = \dfrac{36}{70} = \dfrac{18}{35}$

3) $\dfrac{1}{8} \times \dfrac{1}{2} = \dfrac{1 \times 1}{8 \times 2} = \dfrac{1}{16}$

4) $\dfrac{5}{6} \times \dfrac{2}{10} = \dfrac{5 \times 2}{6 \times 10} = \dfrac{10}{60} = \dfrac{1}{6}$

5) $\dfrac{4}{6} \times \dfrac{2}{7} = \dfrac{4 \times 2}{6 \times 7} = \dfrac{8}{42} = \dfrac{4}{21}$

6) $\dfrac{5}{6} \times \dfrac{1}{3} = \dfrac{5 \times 1}{6 \times 3} = \dfrac{5}{18}$

<h2 style="text-align:center">EXERCISE 17</h2>

1) $\dfrac{3}{10} \times \dfrac{1}{9} = \dfrac{3 \times 1}{10 \times 9} = \dfrac{3}{90} = \dfrac{1}{30}$

2) $\dfrac{4}{6} \times \dfrac{5}{9} = \dfrac{4 \times 5}{6 \times 9} = \dfrac{20}{54} = \dfrac{10}{27}$

3) $\dfrac{5}{9} \times \dfrac{1}{2} = \dfrac{5 \times 1}{9 \times 2} = \dfrac{5}{18}$

4) $\dfrac{3}{5} \times \dfrac{1}{4} = \dfrac{3 \times 1}{5 \times 4} = \dfrac{3}{20}$

5) $\dfrac{6}{7} \times \dfrac{2}{10} = \dfrac{6 \times 2}{7 \times 10} = \dfrac{12}{70} = \dfrac{6}{35}$

6) $\dfrac{6}{7} \times \dfrac{4}{5} = \dfrac{6 \times 4}{7 \times 5} = \dfrac{24}{35}$

<h2 style="text-align:center">EXERCISE 18</h2>

1) $\dfrac{1}{3} \times \dfrac{1}{2} = \dfrac{1 \times 1}{3 \times 2} = \dfrac{1}{6}$

2) $\dfrac{7}{10} \times \dfrac{2}{7} = \dfrac{7 \times 2}{10 \times 7} = \dfrac{14}{70} = \dfrac{1}{5}$

3) $\dfrac{1}{2} \times \dfrac{4}{7} = \dfrac{1 \times 4}{2 \times 7} = \dfrac{4}{14} = \dfrac{2}{7}$

4) $\dfrac{5}{8} \times \dfrac{4}{9} = \dfrac{5 \times 4}{8 \times 9} = \dfrac{20}{72} = \dfrac{5}{18}$

5) $\dfrac{7}{10} \times \dfrac{4}{7} = \dfrac{7 \times 4}{10 \times 7} = \dfrac{28}{70} = \dfrac{2}{5}$

6) $\dfrac{4}{6} \times \dfrac{2}{4} = \dfrac{4 \times 2}{6 \times 4} = \dfrac{8}{24} = \dfrac{1}{3}$

<h2 style="text-align:center">EXERCISE 19</h2>

1) $\dfrac{9}{10} \times \dfrac{2}{3} = \dfrac{9 \times 2}{10 \times 3} = \dfrac{18}{30} = \dfrac{3}{5}$

2) $\dfrac{5}{10} \times \dfrac{3}{7} = \dfrac{5 \times 3}{10 \times 7} = \dfrac{15}{70} = \dfrac{3}{14}$

3) $\dfrac{2}{4} \times \dfrac{1}{2} = \dfrac{2 \times 1}{4 \times 2} = \dfrac{2}{8} = \dfrac{1}{4}$

4) $\dfrac{1}{8} \times \dfrac{5}{10} = \dfrac{1 \times 5}{8 \times 10} = \dfrac{5}{80} = \dfrac{1}{16}$

5) $\dfrac{8}{9} \times \dfrac{1}{2} = \dfrac{8 \times 1}{9 \times 2} = \dfrac{8}{18} = \dfrac{4}{9}$

6) $\dfrac{3}{8} \times \dfrac{4}{9} = \dfrac{3 \times 4}{8 \times 9} = \dfrac{12}{72} = \dfrac{1}{6}$

<h2 style="text-align:center">EXERCISE 20</h2>

1) $\dfrac{3}{4} \times \dfrac{5}{7} = \dfrac{3 \times 5}{4 \times 7} = \dfrac{15}{28}$

2) $\dfrac{3}{6} \times \dfrac{2}{8} = \dfrac{3 \times 2}{6 \times 8} = \dfrac{6}{48} = \dfrac{1}{8}$

3) $\dfrac{1}{3} \times \dfrac{4}{8} = \dfrac{1 \times 4}{3 \times 8} = \dfrac{4}{24} = \dfrac{1}{6}$

4) $\dfrac{2}{3} \times \dfrac{1}{7} = \dfrac{2 \times 1}{3 \times 7} = \dfrac{2}{21}$

5) $\dfrac{3}{4} \times \dfrac{2}{3} = \dfrac{3 \times 2}{4 \times 3} = \dfrac{6}{12} = \dfrac{1}{2}$

6) $\dfrac{2}{4} \times \dfrac{2}{8} = \dfrac{2 \times 2}{4 \times 8} = \dfrac{4}{32} = \dfrac{1}{8}$

EXERCISE 21

1) $\dfrac{8}{9} \times \dfrac{16}{20} = \dfrac{8 \times 16}{9 \times 20} = \dfrac{32}{45}$

2) $\dfrac{11}{18} \times \dfrac{1}{7} = \dfrac{11 \times 1}{18 \times 7} = \dfrac{11}{126}$

3) $\dfrac{3}{4} \times \dfrac{17}{18} = \dfrac{3 \times 17}{4 \times 18} = \dfrac{17}{24}$

4) $\dfrac{5}{6} \times \dfrac{5}{8} = \dfrac{5 \times 5}{6 \times 8} = \dfrac{25}{48}$

5) $\dfrac{11}{12} \times \dfrac{13}{14} = \dfrac{11 \times 13}{12 \times 14} = \dfrac{143}{168}$

6) $\dfrac{1}{8} \times \dfrac{3}{5} = \dfrac{1 \times 3}{8 \times 5} = \dfrac{3}{40}$

EXERCISE 22

1) $\dfrac{7}{12} \times \dfrac{1}{2} = \dfrac{7 \times 1}{12 \times 2} = \dfrac{7}{24}$

2) $\dfrac{1}{7} \times \dfrac{2}{15} = \dfrac{1 \times 2}{7 \times 15} = \dfrac{2}{105}$

3) $\dfrac{7}{18} \times \dfrac{1}{5} = \dfrac{7 \times 1}{18 \times 5} = \dfrac{7}{90}$

4) $\dfrac{8}{18} \times \dfrac{4}{9} = \dfrac{8 \times 4}{18 \times 9} = \dfrac{16}{81}$

5) $\dfrac{5}{8} \times \dfrac{2}{4} = \dfrac{5 \times 2}{8 \times 4} = \dfrac{5}{16}$

6) $\dfrac{1}{2} \times \dfrac{3}{5} = \dfrac{1 \times 3}{2 \times 5} = \dfrac{3}{10}$

EXERCISE 23

1) $\dfrac{7}{14} \times \dfrac{1}{2} = \dfrac{7 \times 1}{14 \times 2} = \dfrac{1}{4}$

2) $\dfrac{1}{3} \times \dfrac{13}{16} = \dfrac{1 \times 13}{3 \times 16} = \dfrac{13}{48}$

3) $\dfrac{4}{8} \times \dfrac{5}{14} = \dfrac{4 \times 5}{8 \times 14} = \dfrac{5}{28}$

4) $\dfrac{1}{2} \times \dfrac{9}{14} = \dfrac{1 \times 9}{2 \times 14} = \dfrac{9}{28}$

5) $\dfrac{1}{2} \times \dfrac{6}{7} = \dfrac{1 \times 6}{2 \times 7} = \dfrac{3}{7}$

6) $\dfrac{3}{18} \times \dfrac{11}{20} = \dfrac{3 \times 11}{18 \times 20} = \dfrac{11}{120}$

EXERCISE 24

1) $\dfrac{2}{4} \times \dfrac{4}{8} = \dfrac{2 \times 4}{4 \times 8} = \dfrac{1}{4}$

2) $\dfrac{4}{5} \times \dfrac{5}{6} = \dfrac{4 \times 5}{5 \times 6} = \dfrac{2}{3}$

3) $\dfrac{1}{2} \times \dfrac{2}{3} = \dfrac{1 \times 2}{2 \times 3} = \dfrac{1}{3}$

4) $\dfrac{14}{20} \times \dfrac{10}{16} = \dfrac{14 \times 10}{20 \times 16} = \dfrac{7}{16}$

5) $\dfrac{1}{4} \times \dfrac{1}{5} = \dfrac{1 \times 1}{4 \times 5} = \dfrac{1}{20}$

6) $\dfrac{14}{16} \times \dfrac{10}{12} = \dfrac{14 \times 10}{16 \times 12} = \dfrac{35}{48}$

EXERCISE 25

1) $\dfrac{19}{20} \times \dfrac{6}{7} = \dfrac{19 \times 6}{20 \times 7} = \dfrac{57}{70}$

2) $\dfrac{1}{3} \times \dfrac{1}{5} = \dfrac{1 \times 1}{3 \times 5} = \dfrac{1}{15}$

3) $\dfrac{9}{10} \times \dfrac{1}{2} = \dfrac{9 \times 1}{10 \times 2} = \dfrac{9}{20}$

4) $\dfrac{5}{9} \times \dfrac{5}{14} = \dfrac{5 \times 5}{9 \times 14} = \dfrac{25}{126}$

5) $\dfrac{6}{14} \times \dfrac{6}{9} = \dfrac{6 \times 6}{14 \times 9} = \dfrac{2}{7}$

6) $\dfrac{6}{9} \times \dfrac{1}{2} = \dfrac{6 \times 1}{9 \times 2} = \dfrac{1}{3}$

EXERCISE 26

1) $\dfrac{3}{10} \times \dfrac{2}{7} = \dfrac{3 \times 2}{10 \times 7} = \dfrac{3}{35}$

2) $\dfrac{2}{5} \times \dfrac{2}{6} = \dfrac{2 \times 2}{5 \times 6} = \dfrac{2}{15}$

3) $\dfrac{2}{5} \times \dfrac{1}{2} = \dfrac{2 \times 1}{5 \times 2} = \dfrac{1}{5}$

4) $\dfrac{1}{2} \times \dfrac{2}{5} = \dfrac{1 \times 2}{2 \times 5} = \dfrac{1}{5}$

5) $\dfrac{1}{2} \times \dfrac{6}{15} = \dfrac{1 \times 6}{2 \times 15} = \dfrac{1}{5}$

6) $\dfrac{1}{2} \times \dfrac{2}{4} = \dfrac{1 \times 2}{2 \times 4} = \dfrac{1}{4}$

EXERCISE 27

1) $\dfrac{2}{3} \times \dfrac{5}{6} = \dfrac{2 \times 5}{3 \times 6} = \dfrac{5}{9}$

2) $\dfrac{11}{14} \times \dfrac{4}{15} = \dfrac{11 \times 4}{14 \times 15} = \dfrac{22}{105}$

3) $\dfrac{3}{14} \times \dfrac{6}{7} = \dfrac{3 \times 6}{14 \times 7} = \dfrac{9}{49}$

4) $\dfrac{1}{10} \times \dfrac{9}{20} = \dfrac{1 \times 9}{10 \times 20} = \dfrac{9}{200}$

5) $\dfrac{8}{16} \times \dfrac{1}{4} = \dfrac{8 \times 1}{16 \times 4} = \dfrac{1}{8}$

6) $\dfrac{13}{18} \times \dfrac{7}{10} = \dfrac{13 \times 7}{18 \times 10} = \dfrac{91}{180}$

EXERCISE 28

1) $\dfrac{6}{12} \times \dfrac{4}{6} = \dfrac{6 \times 4}{12 \times 6} = \dfrac{1}{3}$

2) $\dfrac{6}{7} \times \dfrac{1}{14} = \dfrac{6 \times 1}{7 \times 14} = \dfrac{3}{49}$

3) $\dfrac{2}{4} \times \dfrac{1}{3} = \dfrac{2 \times 1}{4 \times 3} = \dfrac{1}{6}$

4) $\dfrac{3}{10} \times \dfrac{4}{8} = \dfrac{3 \times 4}{10 \times 8} = \dfrac{3}{20}$

5) $\dfrac{13}{15} \times \dfrac{3}{6} = \dfrac{13 \times 3}{15 \times 6} = \dfrac{13}{30}$

6) $\dfrac{1}{3} \times \dfrac{17}{20} = \dfrac{1 \times 17}{3 \times 20} = \dfrac{17}{60}$

EXERCISE 29

1) $\dfrac{7}{8} \times \dfrac{1}{2} = \dfrac{7 \times 1}{8 \times 2} = \dfrac{7}{16}$

2) $\dfrac{4}{18} \times \dfrac{10}{15} = \dfrac{4 \times 10}{18 \times 15} = \dfrac{4}{27}$

3) $\dfrac{6}{7} \times \dfrac{1}{2} = \dfrac{6 \times 1}{7 \times 2} = \dfrac{3}{7}$

4) $\dfrac{3}{6} \times \dfrac{5}{10} = \dfrac{3 \times 5}{6 \times 10} = \dfrac{1}{4}$

5) $\dfrac{3}{4} \times \dfrac{7}{18} = \dfrac{3 \times 7}{4 \times 18} = \dfrac{7}{24}$

6) $\dfrac{4}{6} \times \dfrac{11}{20} = \dfrac{4 \times 11}{6 \times 20} = \dfrac{11}{30}$

EXERCISE 30

1) $\dfrac{1}{2} \times \dfrac{8}{9} = \dfrac{1 \times 8}{2 \times 9} = \dfrac{4}{9}$

2) $\dfrac{1}{7} \times \dfrac{2}{8} = \dfrac{1 \times 2}{7 \times 8} = \dfrac{1}{28}$

3) $\dfrac{12}{14} \times \dfrac{2}{3} = \dfrac{12 \times 2}{14 \times 3} = \dfrac{4}{7}$

4) $\dfrac{1}{2} \times \dfrac{1}{14} = \dfrac{1 \times 1}{2 \times 14} = \dfrac{1}{28}$

5) $\dfrac{7}{20} \times \dfrac{3}{8} = \dfrac{7 \times 3}{20 \times 8} = \dfrac{21}{160}$

6) $\dfrac{2}{3} \times \dfrac{5}{8} = \dfrac{2 \times 5}{3 \times 8} = \dfrac{5}{12}$

DIVIDING FRACTIONS

EXERCISE 3

1) $\dfrac{1}{6} \div \dfrac{1}{9} =$ $\dfrac{1 \times 9}{6 \times 1} =$ $\dfrac{9}{6} =$ $\dfrac{3}{2} =$ $1\dfrac{1}{2}$

2) $\dfrac{1}{5} \div \dfrac{6}{15} =$ $\dfrac{1 \times 15}{5 \times 6} =$ $\dfrac{15}{30} =$ $\dfrac{1}{2}$

3) $\dfrac{2}{3} \div \dfrac{1}{2} =$ $\dfrac{2 \times 2}{3 \times 1} =$ $\dfrac{4}{3} =$ $1\dfrac{1}{3}$

4) $\dfrac{1}{2} \div \dfrac{1}{9} =$ $\dfrac{1 \times 9}{2 \times 1} =$ $\dfrac{9}{2} =$ $4\dfrac{1}{2}$

5) $\dfrac{3}{18} \div \dfrac{1}{2} =$ $\dfrac{3 \times 2}{18 \times 1} =$ $\dfrac{6}{18} =$ $\dfrac{1}{3}$

6) $\dfrac{2}{3} \div \dfrac{11}{16} =$ $\dfrac{2 \times 16}{3 \times 11} =$ $\dfrac{32}{33}$

EXERCISE 1

1) $\dfrac{9}{14} \div \dfrac{5}{7} =$ $\dfrac{9 \times 7}{14 \times 5} =$ $\dfrac{63}{70} =$ $\dfrac{9}{10}$

2) $\dfrac{1}{2} \div \dfrac{1}{3} =$ $\dfrac{1 \times 3}{2 \times 1} =$ $\dfrac{3}{2} =$

3) $\dfrac{6}{16} \div \dfrac{4}{10} =$ $\dfrac{6 \times 10}{16 \times 4} =$ $\dfrac{60}{64} =$ $\dfrac{15}{16}$

4) $\dfrac{7}{15} \div \dfrac{3}{6} =$ $\dfrac{7 \times 6}{15 \times 3} =$ $\dfrac{42}{45} =$ $\dfrac{14}{15}$

5) $\dfrac{8}{14} \div \dfrac{2}{3} =$ $\dfrac{8 \times 3}{14 \times 2} =$ $\dfrac{24}{28} =$ $\dfrac{6}{7}$

6) $\dfrac{3}{4} \div \dfrac{1}{3} =$ $\dfrac{3 \times 3}{4 \times 1} =$ $\dfrac{9}{4} =$

EXERCISE 4

1) $\dfrac{4}{8} \div \dfrac{7}{10} =$ $\dfrac{4 \times 10}{8 \times 7} =$ $\dfrac{40}{56} =$ $\dfrac{5}{7}$

2) $\dfrac{8}{10} \div \dfrac{6}{12} =$ $\dfrac{8 \times 12}{10 \times 6} =$ $\dfrac{96}{60} =$ $\dfrac{8}{5} =$ $1\dfrac{3}{5}$

3) $\dfrac{1}{4} \div \dfrac{6}{7} =$ $\dfrac{1 \times 7}{4 \times 6} =$ $\dfrac{7}{24}$

4) $\dfrac{16}{20} \div \dfrac{1}{8} =$ $\dfrac{16 \times 8}{20 \times 1} =$ $\dfrac{128}{20} =$ $\dfrac{32}{5} =$ $6\dfrac{2}{5}$

5) $\dfrac{7}{9} \div \dfrac{17}{20} =$ $\dfrac{7 \times 20}{9 \times 17} =$ $\dfrac{140}{153}$

6) $\dfrac{14}{15} \div \dfrac{4}{10} =$ $\dfrac{14 \times 10}{15 \times 4} =$ $\dfrac{140}{60} =$ $\dfrac{7}{3} =$ $2\dfrac{1}{3}$

EXERCISE 2

1) $\dfrac{7}{10} \div \dfrac{13}{14} =$ $\dfrac{7 \times 14}{10 \times 13} =$ $\dfrac{98}{130} =$ $\dfrac{49}{65}$

2) $\dfrac{2}{7} \div \dfrac{6}{9} =$ $\dfrac{2 \times 9}{7 \times 6} =$ $\dfrac{18}{42} =$ $\dfrac{3}{7}$

3) $\dfrac{1}{9} \div \dfrac{5}{8} =$ $\dfrac{1 \times 8}{9 \times 5} =$ $\dfrac{8}{45}$

4) $\dfrac{2}{4} \div \dfrac{1}{7} =$ $\dfrac{2 \times 7}{4 \times 1} =$ $\dfrac{14}{4} =$ $\dfrac{7}{2} =$ $3\dfrac{1}{2}$

5) $\dfrac{1}{6} \div \dfrac{1}{3} =$ $\dfrac{1 \times 3}{6 \times 1} =$ $\dfrac{3}{6} =$ $\dfrac{1}{2}$

6) $\dfrac{5}{7} \div \dfrac{19}{20} =$ $\dfrac{5 \times 20}{7 \times 19} =$ $\dfrac{100}{133}$

EXERCISE 5

1) $\dfrac{3}{5} \div \dfrac{1}{4} =$ $\dfrac{3 \times 4}{5 \times 1} =$ $\dfrac{12}{5} =$ $2\dfrac{2}{5}$

2) $\dfrac{2}{9} \div \dfrac{2}{5} =$ $\dfrac{2 \times 5}{9 \times 2} =$ $\dfrac{10}{18} =$ $\dfrac{5}{9}$

3) $\dfrac{6}{15} \div \dfrac{1}{2} =$ $\dfrac{6 \times 2}{15 \times 1} =$ $\dfrac{12}{15} =$ $\dfrac{4}{5}$

4) $\dfrac{9}{12} \div \dfrac{3}{6} =$ $\dfrac{9 \times 6}{12 \times 3} =$ $\dfrac{54}{36} =$ $\dfrac{3}{2} =$ $1\dfrac{1}{2}$

5) $\dfrac{10}{12} \div \dfrac{1}{2} =$ $\dfrac{10 \times 2}{12 \times 1} =$ $\dfrac{20}{12} =$ $\dfrac{5}{3} =$ $1\dfrac{2}{3}$

6) $\dfrac{1}{2} \div \dfrac{1}{20} =$ $\dfrac{1 \times 20}{2 \times 1} =$ $\dfrac{20}{2} =$ $\dfrac{10}{1} =$ $10\dfrac{0}{1}$

EXERCISE 6

1) $\dfrac{7}{9} \div \dfrac{1}{3} = \dfrac{7 \times 3}{9 \times 1} = \dfrac{21}{9} = \dfrac{7}{3} = 2\dfrac{1}{3}$

2) $\dfrac{2}{7} \div \dfrac{2}{4} = \dfrac{2 \times 4}{7 \times 2} = \dfrac{8}{14} = \dfrac{4}{7}$

3) $\dfrac{8}{16} \div \dfrac{16}{18} = \dfrac{8 \times 18}{16 \times 16} = \dfrac{144}{256} = \dfrac{9}{16}$

4) $\dfrac{2}{10} \div \dfrac{1}{14} = \dfrac{2 \times 14}{10 \times 1} = \dfrac{28}{10} = \dfrac{14}{5} = 2\dfrac{4}{5}$

5) $\dfrac{7}{12} \div \dfrac{8}{16} = \dfrac{7 \times 16}{12 \times 8} = \dfrac{112}{96} = \dfrac{7}{6} = 1\dfrac{1}{6}$

6) $\dfrac{2}{3} \div \dfrac{1}{4} = \dfrac{2 \times 4}{3 \times 1} = \dfrac{8}{3} = 2\dfrac{2}{3}$

EXERCISE 7

1) $\dfrac{1}{16} \div \dfrac{3}{8} = \dfrac{1 \times 8}{16 \times 3} = \dfrac{8}{48} = \dfrac{1}{6}$

2) $\dfrac{1}{8} \div \dfrac{5}{14} = \dfrac{1 \times 14}{8 \times 5} = \dfrac{14}{40} = \dfrac{7}{20}$

3) $\dfrac{5}{6} \div \dfrac{3}{5} = \dfrac{5 \times 5}{6 \times 3} = \dfrac{25}{18} = 1\dfrac{7}{18}$

4) $\dfrac{2}{6} \div \dfrac{1}{2} = \dfrac{2 \times 2}{6 \times 1} = \dfrac{4}{6} = \dfrac{2}{3}$

5) $\dfrac{6}{12} \div \dfrac{3}{7} = \dfrac{6 \times 7}{12 \times 3} = \dfrac{42}{36} = \dfrac{7}{6} = 1\dfrac{1}{6}$

6) $\dfrac{1}{3} \div \dfrac{4}{8} = \dfrac{1 \times 8}{3 \times 4} = \dfrac{8}{12} = \dfrac{2}{3}$

EXERCISE 8

1) $\dfrac{7}{8} \div \dfrac{6}{9} = \dfrac{7 \times 9}{8 \times 6} = \dfrac{63}{48} = \dfrac{21}{16} = 1\dfrac{5}{16}$

2) $\dfrac{7}{14} \div \dfrac{3}{8} = \dfrac{7 \times 8}{14 \times 3} = \dfrac{56}{42} = \dfrac{4}{3} = 1\dfrac{1}{3}$

3) $\dfrac{2}{14} \div \dfrac{4}{8} = \dfrac{2 \times 8}{14 \times 4} = \dfrac{16}{56} = \dfrac{2}{7}$

4) $\dfrac{10}{18} \div \dfrac{5}{12} = \dfrac{10 \times 12}{18 \times 5} = \dfrac{120}{90} = \dfrac{4}{3} = 1\dfrac{1}{3}$

5) $\dfrac{9}{10} \div \dfrac{6}{12} = \dfrac{9 \times 12}{10 \times 6} = \dfrac{108}{60} = \dfrac{9}{5} = 1\dfrac{4}{5}$

6) $\dfrac{7}{16} \div \dfrac{3}{4} = \dfrac{7 \times 4}{16 \times 3} = \dfrac{28}{48} = \dfrac{7}{12}$

EXERCISE 9

1) $\dfrac{2}{4} \div \dfrac{3}{14} = \dfrac{2 \times 14}{4 \times 3} = \dfrac{28}{12} = \dfrac{7}{3} = 2\dfrac{1}{3}$

2) $\dfrac{1}{6} \div \dfrac{17}{18} = \dfrac{1 \times 18}{6 \times 17} = \dfrac{18}{102} = \dfrac{3}{17}$

3) $\dfrac{5}{8} \div \dfrac{2}{14} = \dfrac{5 \times 14}{8 \times 2} = \dfrac{70}{16} = \dfrac{35}{8} = 4\dfrac{3}{8}$

4) $\dfrac{1}{5} \div \dfrac{1}{7} = \dfrac{1 \times 7}{5 \times 1} = \dfrac{7}{5} = 1\dfrac{2}{5}$

5) $\dfrac{2}{3} \div \dfrac{3}{16} = \dfrac{2 \times 16}{3 \times 3} = \dfrac{32}{9} = 3\dfrac{5}{9}$

6) $\dfrac{15}{16} \div \dfrac{3}{5} = \dfrac{15 \times 5}{16 \times 3} = \dfrac{75}{48} = \dfrac{25}{16} = 1\dfrac{9}{16}$

EXERCISE 10

1) $\dfrac{13}{14} \div \dfrac{1}{2} = \dfrac{13 \times 2}{14 \times 1} = \dfrac{26}{14} = \dfrac{13}{7} = 1\dfrac{6}{7}$

2) $\dfrac{12}{14} \div \dfrac{1}{2} = \dfrac{12 \times 2}{14 \times 1} = \dfrac{24}{14} = \dfrac{12}{7} = 1\dfrac{5}{7}$

3) $\dfrac{1}{2} \div \dfrac{13}{15} = \dfrac{1 \times 15}{2 \times 13} = \dfrac{15}{26}$

4) $\dfrac{1}{16} \div \dfrac{4}{10} = \dfrac{1 \times 10}{16 \times 4} = \dfrac{10}{64} = \dfrac{5}{32}$

5) $\dfrac{1}{4} \div \dfrac{5}{12} = \dfrac{1 \times 12}{4 \times 5} = \dfrac{12}{20} = \dfrac{3}{5}$

6) $\dfrac{7}{20} \div \dfrac{1}{2} = \dfrac{7 \times 2}{20 \times 1} = \dfrac{14}{20} = \dfrac{7}{10}$

EXERCISE 11

1) $\dfrac{9}{15} \div \dfrac{6}{7} = \dfrac{9 \times 7}{15 \times 6} = \dfrac{63}{90} = \dfrac{7}{10}$

2) $\dfrac{8}{9} \div \dfrac{1}{3} = \dfrac{8 \times 3}{9 \times 1} = \dfrac{24}{9} = \dfrac{8}{3} = 2\dfrac{2}{3}$

3) $\dfrac{2}{7} \div \dfrac{2}{8} = \dfrac{2 \times 8}{7 \times 2} = \dfrac{16}{14} = \dfrac{8}{7} = 1\dfrac{1}{7}$

4) $\dfrac{2}{12} \div \dfrac{4}{6} = \dfrac{2 \times 6}{12 \times 4} = \dfrac{12}{48} = \dfrac{1}{4}$

5) $\dfrac{5}{12} \div \dfrac{4}{8} = \dfrac{5 \times 8}{12 \times 4} = \dfrac{40}{48} = \dfrac{5}{6}$

6) $\dfrac{7}{8} \div \dfrac{2}{3} = \dfrac{7 \times 3}{8 \times 2} = \dfrac{21}{16} = 1\dfrac{5}{16}$

EXERCISE 12

1) $\dfrac{5}{10} \div \dfrac{4}{7} = \dfrac{5 \times 7}{10 \times 4} = \dfrac{35}{40} = \dfrac{7}{8}$

2) $\dfrac{1}{2} \div \dfrac{12}{16} = \dfrac{1 \times 16}{2 \times 12} = \dfrac{16}{24} = \dfrac{2}{3}$

3) $\dfrac{3}{9} \div \dfrac{4}{10} = \dfrac{3 \times 10}{9 \times 4} = \dfrac{30}{36} = \dfrac{5}{6}$

4) $\dfrac{2}{15} \div \dfrac{1}{5} = \dfrac{2 \times 5}{15 \times 1} = \dfrac{10}{15} = \dfrac{2}{3}$

5) $\dfrac{6}{9} \div \dfrac{2}{4} = \dfrac{6 \times 4}{9 \times 2} = \dfrac{24}{18} = \dfrac{4}{3} = 1\dfrac{1}{3}$

6) $\dfrac{1}{3} \div \dfrac{6}{8} = \dfrac{1 \times 8}{3 \times 6} = \dfrac{8}{18} = \dfrac{4}{9}$

EXERCISE 13

1) $\dfrac{17}{20} \div \dfrac{1}{3} = \dfrac{17 \times 3}{20 \times 1} = \dfrac{51}{20} = 2\dfrac{11}{20}$

2) $\dfrac{1}{2} \div \dfrac{5}{6} = \dfrac{1 \times 6}{2 \times 5} = \dfrac{6}{10} = \dfrac{3}{5}$

3) $\dfrac{1}{8} \div \dfrac{6}{12} = \dfrac{1 \times 12}{8 \times 6} = \dfrac{12}{48} = \dfrac{1}{4}$

4) $\dfrac{14}{16} \div \dfrac{2}{5} = \dfrac{14 \times 5}{16 \times 2} = \dfrac{70}{32} = \dfrac{35}{16} = 2\dfrac{3}{16}$

5) $\dfrac{12}{15} \div \dfrac{3}{14} = \dfrac{12 \times 14}{15 \times 3} = \dfrac{168}{45} = \dfrac{56}{15} = 3\dfrac{11}{15}$

6) $\dfrac{5}{16} \div \dfrac{1}{4} = \dfrac{5 \times 4}{16 \times 1} = \dfrac{20}{16} = \dfrac{5}{4} = 1\dfrac{1}{4}$

EXERCISE 14

1) $\dfrac{4}{6} \div \dfrac{13}{16} = \dfrac{4 \times 16}{6 \times 13} = \dfrac{64}{78} = \dfrac{32}{39}$

2) $\dfrac{3}{6} \div \dfrac{4}{9} = \dfrac{3 \times 9}{6 \times 4} = \dfrac{27}{24} = \dfrac{9}{8} = 1\dfrac{1}{8}$

3) $\dfrac{7}{15} \div \dfrac{9}{10} = \dfrac{7 \times 10}{15 \times 9} = \dfrac{70}{135} = \dfrac{14}{27}$

4) $\dfrac{14}{18} \div \dfrac{1}{12} = \dfrac{14 \times 12}{18 \times 1} = \dfrac{168}{18} = \dfrac{28}{3} = 9\dfrac{1}{3}$

5) $\dfrac{9}{14} \div \dfrac{1}{12} = \dfrac{9 \times 12}{14 \times 1} = \dfrac{108}{14} = \dfrac{54}{7} = 7\dfrac{5}{7}$

6) $\dfrac{11}{16} \div \dfrac{8}{10} = \dfrac{11 \times 10}{16 \times 8} = \dfrac{110}{128} = \dfrac{55}{64}$

EXERCISE 15

1) $\dfrac{18}{20} \div \dfrac{8}{15} = \dfrac{18 \times 15}{20 \times 8} = \dfrac{270}{160} = \dfrac{27}{16} = 1\dfrac{11}{16}$

2) $\dfrac{6}{20} \div \dfrac{3}{4} = \dfrac{6 \times 4}{20 \times 3} = \dfrac{24}{60} = \dfrac{2}{5}$

3) $\dfrac{4}{9} \div \dfrac{1}{14} = \dfrac{4 \times 14}{9 \times 1} = \dfrac{56}{9} = 6\dfrac{2}{9}$

4) $\dfrac{1}{6} \div \dfrac{6}{8} = \dfrac{1 \times 8}{6 \times 6} = \dfrac{8}{36} = \dfrac{2}{9}$

5) $\dfrac{12}{20} \div \dfrac{1}{16} = \dfrac{12 \times 16}{20 \times 1} = \dfrac{192}{20} = \dfrac{48}{5} = 9\dfrac{3}{5}$

6) $\dfrac{1}{6} \div \dfrac{7}{9} = \dfrac{1 \times 9}{6 \times 7} = \dfrac{9}{42} = \dfrac{3}{14}$

EXERCISE 16

1) $\dfrac{1}{6} \div \dfrac{18}{20} = \dfrac{1 \times 20}{6 \times 18} = \dfrac{20}{108} = \dfrac{5}{27}$

2) $\dfrac{7}{14} \div \dfrac{12}{15} = \dfrac{7 \times 15}{14 \times 12} = \dfrac{105}{168} = \dfrac{5}{8}$

3) $\dfrac{1}{6} \div \dfrac{4}{12} = \dfrac{1 \times 12}{6 \times 4} = \dfrac{12}{24} = \dfrac{1}{2}$

4) $\dfrac{2}{8} \div \dfrac{2}{9} = \dfrac{2 \times 9}{8 \times 2} = \dfrac{18}{16} = \dfrac{9}{8} = 1\dfrac{1}{8}$

5) $\dfrac{5}{6} \div \dfrac{8}{9} = \dfrac{5 \times 9}{6 \times 8} = \dfrac{45}{48} = \dfrac{15}{16}$

6) $\dfrac{8}{15} \div \dfrac{1}{2} = \dfrac{8 \times 2}{15 \times 1} = \dfrac{16}{15} = 1\dfrac{1}{15}$

EXERCISE 17

1) $\dfrac{5}{12} \div \dfrac{1}{6} = \dfrac{5 \times 6}{12 \times 1} = \dfrac{30}{12} = \dfrac{5}{2} = 2\dfrac{1}{2}$

2) $\dfrac{3}{16} \div \dfrac{5}{10} = \dfrac{3 \times 10}{16 \times 5} = \dfrac{30}{80} = \dfrac{3}{8}$

3) $\dfrac{6}{10} \div \dfrac{2}{6} = \dfrac{6 \times 6}{10 \times 2} = \dfrac{36}{20} = \dfrac{9}{5} = 1\dfrac{4}{5}$

4) $\dfrac{1}{10} \div \dfrac{2}{7} = \dfrac{1 \times 7}{10 \times 2} = \dfrac{7}{20}$

5) $\dfrac{3}{5} \div \dfrac{4}{6} = \dfrac{3 \times 6}{5 \times 4} = \dfrac{18}{20} = \dfrac{9}{10}$

6) $\dfrac{7}{9} \div \dfrac{17}{20} = \dfrac{7 \times 20}{9 \times 17} = \dfrac{140}{153}$

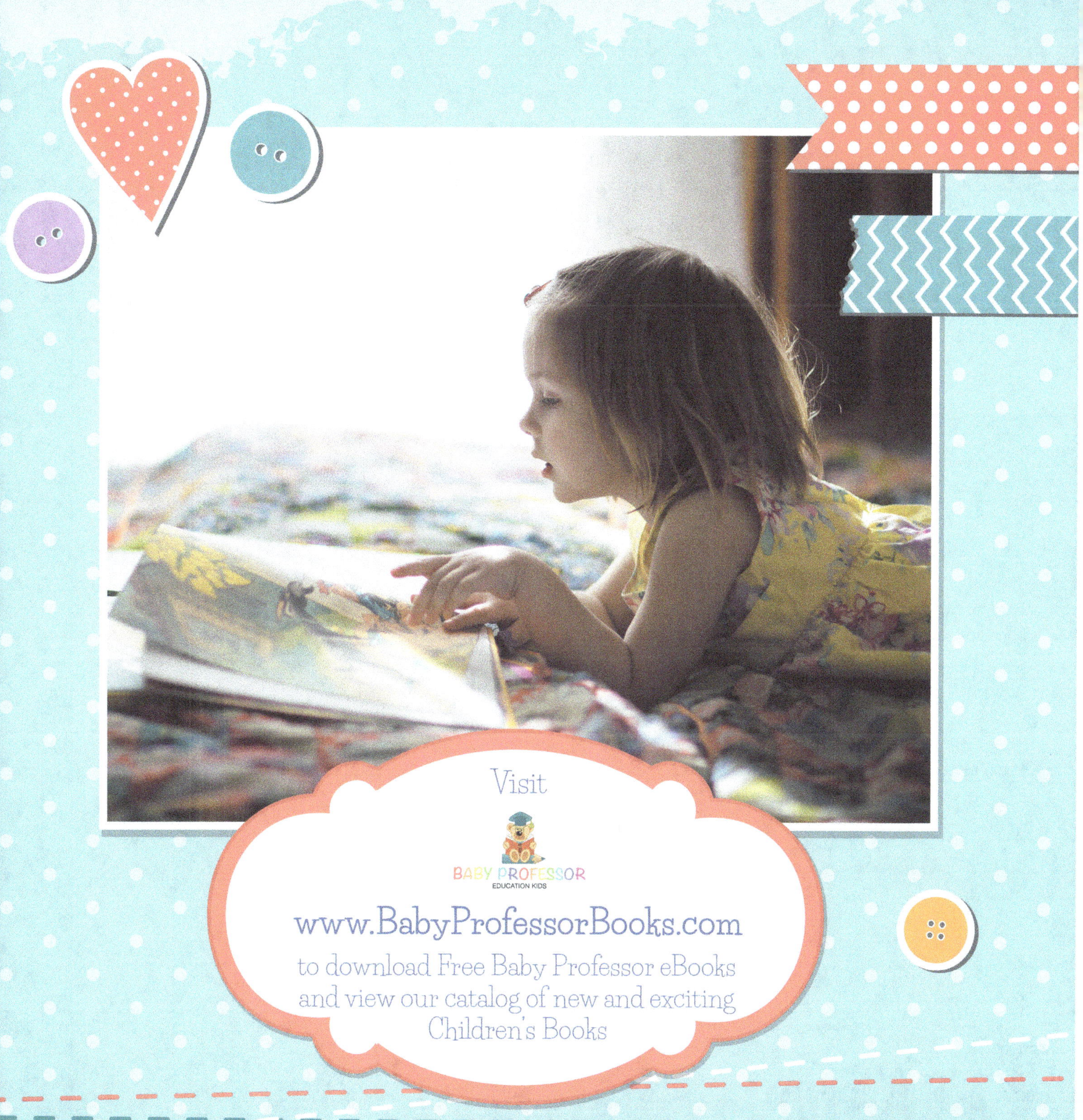
Visit

BABY PROFESSOR
EDUCATION KIDS

www.BabyProfessorBooks.com

to download Free Baby Professor eBooks
and view our catalog of new and exciting
Children's Books